Z99

READING!
ROCKS!

WINSTON
CHURCHILL
BRITISH SOLDIER, WRITER, STATESMAN

Thanks
for having
us!
Z99 Reading, OO
Rocks
Erick   "EP"

To: Jack
Happy Reading!
Margo
WM

From: WM

SPECIAL LIVES IN HISTORY THAT BECOME

Signature LIVES

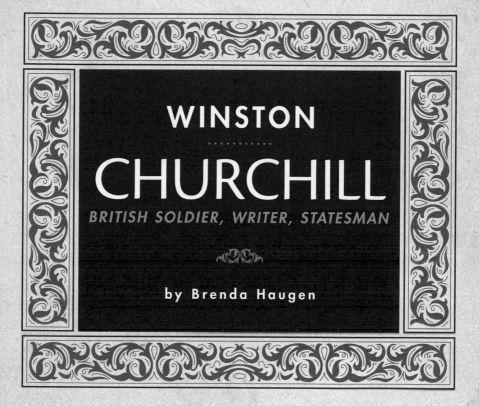

WINSTON
CHURCHILL
BRITISH SOLDIER, WRITER, STATESMAN

by Brenda Haugen

Content Adviser: Edward Segel, Ph.D.,
Professor of History and Humanities,
Reed College

Reading Adviser: Rosemary G. Palmer, Ph.D.,
Department of Literacy, College of Education,
Boise State University

COMPASS POINT BOOKS ✦ MINNEAPOLIS, MINNESOTA

Compass Point Books
3109 West 50th Street, #115
Minneapolis, MN 55410

Visit Compass Point Books on the Internet at *www.compasspointbooks.com*
or e-mail your request to *custserv@compasspointbooks.com*

Editor: Jennifer VanVoorst
Page Production: Noumenon Creative
Photo Researcher: Svetlana Zhurkin
Cartographer: XNR Productions, Inc.
Library Consultant: Kathleen Baxter

Art Director: Jaime Martens
Creative Director: Keith Griffin
Editorial Director: Carol Jones
Managing Editor: Catherine Neitge

For Marianne Cassels. BLH

Library of Congress Cataloging-in-Publication Data
Haugen, Brenda.
  Winston Churchill : British soldier, writer, statesman / by Brenda Haugen.
     p. cm. — (Signature lives)
  Includes bibliographical references and index.
  ISBN 0-7565-1582-3
  1. Churchill, Winston, Sir, 1874–1965—Juvenile literature. 2. Great
Britain—Politics and government—20th century—Juvenile literature. 3.
Prime ministers—Great Britain—Biography—Juvenile literature. 4. World
War, 1939–1945—Great Britain—Juvenile literature. I. Title. II. Series.
  DA566.9.C5H29 2006
  941.084'092—dc22   2005028707

Signature Lives

MODERN WORLD

From 1900 to the present day, humanity and the world have undergone major changes. New political ideas resulted in worldwide wars. Fascism and communism divided some countries, and democracy brought others together. Drastic shifts in theories and practice tested the standards of personal freedoms and religious conventions as well as science, technology, and industry. These changes have created a need for world policies and an understanding of international relations. The new mind-set of the modern world includes a focus on humanitarianism and the belief that a global economy has made the world a more connected place.

Winston Churchill

Table of Contents

1 DESTINED TO LEAD

Prime Minister Winston Churchill's powerful voice echoed throughout the hall that housed Great Britain's House of Commons. Defiantly, he told his nation:

> I have nothing to offer but blood, toil, tears, and sweat. You ask, "What is our policy?" I will say: it is to wage war, by sea, land, and air, with all our might and with all the strength that God can give us. ... You ask, "What is our aim?" I can answer in one word: Victory—victory at all costs, victory in spite of terror; victory, however long and hard the road may be; for without victory there is no survival.

Ever since the end of World War I, Churchill had

Prime Minister Winston Churchill flashed supporters the "V for Victory" sign at the end of World War II.

been warning his nation of the danger of German rearmament, but no one had taken his message seriously. Though events had proven him right, it gave him no satisfaction. Now Great Britain needed his leadership: World War II was under way.

When Churchill delivered his famous speech in 1940, he was just three days into his term as prime minister. Instead of feeling overwhelmed or frightened, however, he felt relieved. He had cheated death many times in the past and had always believed it was because he had a great destiny yet to be fulfilled. Now he knew: He was meant to lead Great Britain through World War II. "I felt as if I were walking with destiny, and that all my past life had been but a preparation for this hour and for this trial," Churchill said.

Churchill was known not only for his powerful speeches, but also for his clever way with words. He often used his wit to comment on his career. Churchill said, "In war, you can only be killed once, but in politics, many times." He also commented, "History will be kind to me for I intend to write it."

At 65 years old, Churchill had already accomplished much with his life. He had been a soldier, a journalist, an author, and a politician, but his greatest achievement was yet to come. To guide his country through World War II was his destiny, and he led his nation with great conviction. And as Germany pounded England with bombs, it often seemed that Churchill's resolve was the only

Churchill was joined by Queen Elizabeth and King George VI during a victory celebration in England.

thing keeping Great Britain going. By his words and his leadership, he would guide his country—along with the United States and the Soviet Union—to victory in World War II. And in doing so, he would become one of the most celebrated figures of the 20th century. ♖

2 A YOUNG REBEL

∾⬥∾

From the moment he was born, Winston Churchill made it clear he'd do things his own way and on his own time schedule.

Winston's parents—Lord Randolph Churchill and his wife Jennie—met in the summer of 1873. Jennie Jerome grew up in a wealthy American family and was visiting England with her mother. When Randolph met the beautiful young woman, he immediately fell in love with her. A few months later, Randolph and Jennie were married.

The couple lived in Blenheim Palace near Oxfordshire, England, the home of Randolph's father, the seventh Duke of Marlborough. On November 30, 1874, Jennie insisted on going to a ball at the palace though she was several months pregnant. Her due

Winston Churchill was 7 years old when he left home to attend St. James's School.

date was weeks away, and she didn't want to miss out on the fun.

During the ball, Jennie suddenly felt faint and was quietly whisked off to a coatroom to recover. Instead, she gave birth to her first son, Winston Spencer Churchill.

Like most children born into privileged families in England, Winston was raised by nurses. Because Winston could be stubborn and mischievous, many of his nurses quit in frustration. He met his match, however, in Mrs. Everest, who would become like family to the youngster. Mrs. Everest gave Winston the love and security he didn't get from his parents.

Lord Randolph Churchill (1849–1895)

Still, it wasn't the same. Though Winston loved Mrs. Everest, he wouldn't remember his childhood fondly.

But that didn't mean Winston didn't love his parents. He just always felt a distance between himself and them. He looked up to his father, a well-respected politician in whose footsteps he would eventually follow. However, they spent little time together while Winston was growing up.

Winston thought of his mother almost as a fairy-tale princess. He wrote, "She shone for me like the evening star. I loved her dearly but at a distance." His mother's busy social life meant that she was rarely around.

When Winston was 2 years old, his grandfather was

Jennie Jerome Churchill (1854–1921)

appointed lord lieutenant of Ireland, and the whole family moved to Dublin. Winston's father worked as an unpaid secretary for the boy's grandfather, who lived in a grand lodge. Winston and his parents lived in a smaller lodge a few hundred feet away. Winston later wrote:

> *It was at "The Little Lodge" I was first menaced with Education. The approach of a sinister figure described as "the Governess" was announced. Her arrival was fixed for a certain day. In order to prepare ... Mrs. Everest produced a book called* Reading Without Tears. *It certainly did not justify its title in my case.*

> *Winston's father, Lord Randolph Churchill, was a famous and controversial figure in British politics. He served as chancellor of the exchequer (similar to the U.S. secretary of the treasury), was a reforming figure in the Conservative government, and later a rebel against party discipline. Lord Randolph's career became an important model for his son, and Winston followed in his father's footsteps by holding a number of positions and views that his father had held.*

Winston found learning difficult. He spoke with a stutter and a lisp, and his high spirits made it difficult for him to pay attention. He dreaded the arrival of his governess, who served as his teacher, and hid when he learned she was coming. But Winston's hiding place in the woods was soon discovered, and his education began.

In 1880, Winston's grandfather, a member of the Conservative Party, was replaced in Ireland when the Liberals came to power, and the Churchills moved back to their palace in England.

In February of that year, Winston's brother, John, was born. Because of the nearly six-year age difference, they didn't grow up being very close. And after Winston was sent to a boarding school called St. James's the following year, the boys spent even less time together. Winston was afraid of being away from home, but he also felt excited about living with other boys his own age and making some new friends.

Arriving at St. James's School, Winston and his mother were impressed with the swimming pool

Winston (right) and his brother, John, were not close, but they both adored their mother, Jennie.

and playground. His parents hoped this inviting atmosphere would lead Winston to enjoy learning. But the school's friendly appearance was misleading. Rules at the school were strict, and misbehavior was handled with a flogging, a punishment Winston often suffered.

Once the language of
the Roman Empire,
Latin was spoken in
Western Europe for
hundreds of years.
Though many English
words got their start in
the Latin language, it
has not been a spoken
language since the
1500s. Latin remains
the official language of
the Roman Catholic
Church, but its churches
throughout the world
rarely use it today.

Winston's first day of class involved learning Latin, which proved difficult for him. He could not understand the need for Latin—or for several of his other classes, either. If he didn't see the value in a class, he refused to learn. He recalled:

How I hated this school, and what a life of anxiety I lived there for more than two years. I made very little progress at my lessons, and none at all at games. I counted the days and the hours to the end of every term, when I should return home from this hateful servitude.

After two years at St. James's School, Winston fell ill, and his parents brought him back home to get well. Once he had recovered, the Churchills decided to enroll him in Brighton instead. Run by two kindly women, Brighton became both Winston's school and home from 1880 to 1883.

At Brighton, Winston recalled, "I was allowed to learn things that interested me." Still he struggled, particularly in Latin and math. When the time came for him to take the entrance exam for Harrow, a leading

Blenheim Palace, in central England, was Winston's childhood home.

English secondary school, Winston discovered he couldn't answer a single question on the Latin test. After two hours, an usher collected the papers and handed them to the Harrow headmaster, Dr. Welldon. He looked at what Winston had done—or hadn't done—and chose to pass him anyway. Winston said he'd always respected Dr. Welldon for looking past the test and giving him a chance.

Winston posed for a formal portrait while a student at Harrow.

Winston studied at Harrow for four-and-a-half years, but he continued to refuse to learn anything unless he saw how it would be useful. The three years he spent in army class, however, were different. Ever since he was small, Winston was interested in the military. In fact, he owned a set of toy soldiers that eventually numbered about 1,500. He'd battle against his brother's troops in pretend wars. But now, as a young man, he hoped his education would help him gain entrance to the Royal Military College at Sandhurst. His father believed that a soldier's life was the best career his son, whom he thought to be of limited intelligence, could hope for. However, Winston's difficulty in passing entrance exams would plague him yet again. ☙

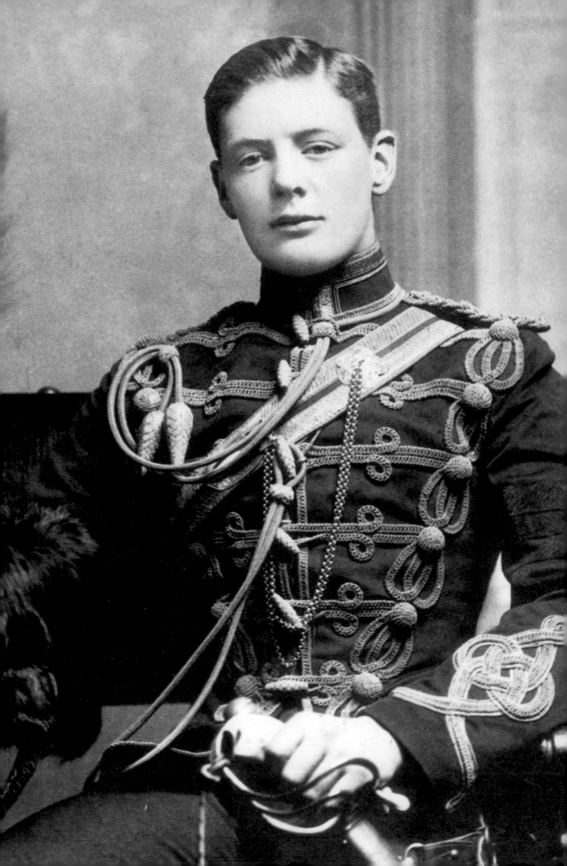

3 PREPARING FOR MILITARY LIFE

❧❦❧

The thought of surrendering never crossed Winston Churchill's mind. As his brother, John, and a cousin chased him in a game of hounds and deer, Churchill—the deer—managed to avoid capture. But after 20 minutes of evading the hounds, Churchill gasped for breath and decided to cross a bridge. He quickly found himself trapped in the center of the 50-yard (46-meter) expanse. His cousin stood on one end of the bridge and his brother on the other.

The three were visiting their aunt, Lady Wimborne, on her 40-acre (16-hectare) estate near Bournemouth in January 1893. Churchill had recently failed the entrance exam for the Royal Military Academy at Sandhurst. He was taking a short vacation before meeting with a tutor in London and trying again to

At 19 years old, Winston Churchill became a member of the 4th Hussars, a famed British military unit.

pass the test.

Churchill loved the outdoors, and staying on his aunt's estate renewed his spirit. The bridge he now stood on spanned a deep ravine that ran through the wilderness about 30 feet (9 m) below. The ravine was dotted with huge, green pine trees that seemed to almost touch the bridge.

As his brother and cousin closed the gap, Churchill should have given up, but that wasn't in his nature. With no other way to escape, Churchill decided he would jump from the bridge onto the top of one of the tall pine trees and shimmy down to the ground. However, the trees were farther away than they appeared. Churchill missed the tree he aimed for and hit the ground hard.

He remained unconscious for three days, but his family counted themselves lucky he was still alive. He suffered many injuries, including a ruptured kidney. Churchill's father came to Bournemouth with the best surgeon in England. He was able to repair the damage, but Churchill's recovery would prove to be a long journey. He remained bedridden for three months, and full recovery took nearly a year.

This incident and other brushes with death never cured Churchill of his desire for adventure. He also became known for not giving in, even when the odds didn't appear to be in his favor. He didn't give up on getting into Sandhurst either. On his third try,

Churchill finally passed the entrance exam.

An excited Churchill wrote to his father about qualifying for the cavalry, a military unit that fought on horseback. To his surprise, Winston discovered his father was disappointed he hadn't scored high enough to join the infantry. Being a part of the cavalry cost a great deal more than being a part of the infantry,

Churchill (left) posed with class-mates at the Royal Military Academy at Sandhurst.

mainly because cavalrymen were burdened with buying and caring for the horses they rode. Owning horses was one of the reasons Churchill found the cavalry so exciting, though his father only saw the added expense.

Churchill worked harder at his studies at Sandhurst than he had at previous schools. He was happy to discover he wouldn't have to suffer through Latin and math again. His classes included mapmaking, tactics, military administration, military law, and fortification. He also participated in drill, riding, and gymnastics. With this full schedule, Churchill always felt tired at the end of the day. But he enjoyed school for the first time, and it showed in his grades. For the first time, Churchill wasn't near the very bottom of his class. In 1894, he graduated eighth out of a class of 150.

England's Royal Military Academy at Sandhurst continues to train young men and women for service in the British army. It is the British equivalent of the U.S. Military Academy at West Point.

Churchill traveled home in December to await his military assignment. He was still there when his father died on January 24, 1895. Though only 45, Randolph had been seriously ill for about a year. While his father's death came as no surprise, Churchill mourned that he would never get to be as close to Randolph as he had always hoped.

"All my dreams of comradeship

Students played cricket on the grounds of the Royal Military Academy at Sandhurst.

with him, of entering Parliament at his side and in his support, were ended," Churchill later wrote. "There remained for me only to pursue his aim and vindicate his memory."

His relationship with his mother, however, did change. Jennie became more involved in his life and used her influence to help her son whenever she could. Churchill recalled:

> *She was still at forty young, beautiful and fascinating. We worked together on even terms, more like brother and sister than mother and son. At least so it seemed to me. And so it continued until the end.*

In March 1895, Churchill was assigned as a lieutenant with the 4th Hussars, a famous fighting unit known for its tough training and strict discipline. For the first six months, the new officers were sent to riding school. Training proved tougher than anything Churchill had yet experienced, but it paid off. He became an excellent horseman. He also developed a love of polo. He invested in the best polo ponies he could buy and played the game whenever possible.

During his training, however, Churchill took time

Churchill became an excellent horseman and enjoyed playing polo.

off to visit Mrs. Everest. Now living with her sister's family in North London, his former nurse was gravely ill. Churchill knew she was dying and was touched that she still worried about him. He later recalled:

> *She knew she was in danger, but her only anxiety was for me. There had been a heavy shower of rain. My jacket was wet. When she felt it with her hands she was greatly alarmed for fear I should catch cold. The jacket had to be taken off and thoroughly dried before she was calm again.*

Churchill hired doctors to care for Mrs. Everest in her final days, and he was at her bedside when she died. For the rest of his life, Churchill would remember the difficulties she suffered in her old age. He would become a champion for the poor and push for pensions and affordable health care for the elderly.

After Mrs. Everest's death, Churchill returned to duty. In 1896, the 4th Hussars were expected to head to India, the cornerstone of the British Empire. Troops spent several years at a time there before their service was complete. Because they would be gone so long, the troops were granted time off before sailing to India. Unlike most of the other troops, Churchill decided to live dangerously during part of his vacation. ☙

4 CHAPTER CORRESPONDENT AND SOLDIER

❧❧❧

Like many other British soldiers, Churchill hungered for adventure, but he wasn't finding it yet in the military. He hoped to find it, however, in Cuba.

Churchill made plans to cover Cuba's fight for independence from Spain for London's *Daily Graphic.* He expected to earn enough as a war correspondent to pay for his trip to Cuba. Churchill traveled with Spanish troops through the Cuban wilderness, which provided plenty of places for the rebels to hide. The Cubans fought guerrilla-style— taking a few shots from the thick cover of the woods and then disappearing. Attacks could come at any time.

On one occasion, Cuban rebels began firing at Churchill and his group after they had bathed in a

about history, government, and philosophy, and he particularly enjoyed books of quotations. He even began writing books himself, including a novel about a revolutionary.

In 1898, Churchill secured a leave from India and headed to the Sudan where a revolution had erupted. A British general allowed Churchill to serve as an extra lieutenant as long as he agreed to pay his own way to Cairo, Egypt, where his regiment was stationed. Agreeing to the terms, Churchill again made arrangements to serve as a war correspondent to cover his costs.

When Churchill got to Egypt, he discovered

At the turn of the 20th century, Great Britain had colonies in most regions of the world.

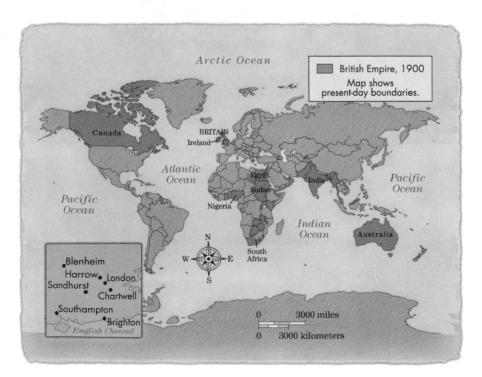

he'd arrived just in time to see some action. His regiment was heading to the fighting front in Sudan. It was a difficult journey, but Churchill did not complain. The troops traveled up the Nile River under the blazing African sun. As the boats transporting the troops came upon rapids, the soldiers were forced to get out of the watercrafts, march around the rapids, and board other boats waiting for them on the other side.

Churchill found the trip to be worth the pain. In September, he participated in the Battle of Omdurman. It proved to be a decisive skirmish in the war and the last cavalry charge in British history. Here, Churchill's old shoulder injury was a blessing in disguise. He wrote:

Once again I was on the hard, crisp desert, my horse at a trot. ... Straight before me a man threw himself on the ground. ... I saw the gleam of his curved sword as he drew it back for a ham-stringing cut. ... I fixed two shots into him at about three yards. As I straightened myself in the saddle, I saw before me another figure with uplifted sword. I raised my pistol and fired. So close were we that the pistol itself actually struck

Lying along the west side of the Nile River, Omdurman stands as a holy city for area Muslims. It also ranks as Sudan's largest city, boasting a population of around 2 million. Across the Nile from Omdurman is Sudan's capital, Khartoum.

*him. Man and sword disappeared below
and behind me.*

*A British light
cavalry unit
cleared the way
to Omdurman,
despite strong
resistance.*

Had Churchill's injured shoulder allowed him
to use the standard cavalry saber instead of a gun,

he likely couldn't have fought off two such quick attacks. His injury may actually have saved his life.

While Churchill escaped injury, his fellow officer Dick Molyneux wasn't so lucky. Molyneux suffered a severe cut above his right wrist that severed all the muscles.

The doctor tending to Molyneux quickly realized a skin graft was needed to save the man's arm. The doctor told a nurse to bare her arm, but as he got ready to cut a piece of her skin for the graft, she turned a very pale shade of white. Instead of risking a fainting nurse, the doctor turned to Churchill and told him to bare his arm. Churchill didn't hesitate. He remembered:

> *[The doctor] then proceeded to cut a piece of skin and some flesh about the size of a shilling from the inside of my forearm. I managed to hold out until he had cut a beautiful piece of skin with a thin layer of flesh attached to it. This precious fragment was then grafted on to my friend's wound. It remains to this day and did him lasting good in many ways. I for my part keep the scar as a souvenir.*

Despite the many adventures the military had offered, Churchill resigned from the army in the spring of 1899 and returned to England to try his hand at politics. But after losing his bid for Parliament, he again sought work as a correspondent. When the *Morning Post*, a London newspaper, offered him $1,000 a month and expenses to cover South Africa's Boer War, he jumped at the chance. Winston Churchill never turned down the opportunity to take part in a war. And with the newspaper's generous offer, he ranked as the highest paid war correspondent in history.

Once in South Africa, Churchill made plans to travel to the fighting front. On his way, he found a small group of British soldiers faced with being severed from other British forces by the Boers. The British commander planned to send an armored train to a town about 40 miles (64 kilometers) north where a large British force also was fighting the Boers. The troops sent to protect the train asked Churchill to join them on their journey. Thinking the adventure would make a great newspaper article, Churchill agreed to go along.

The train pulled away from the station on November 15. For the first 14 miles (22 km) of the trip, the train encountered no problems.

In October 1899, discord erupted into war in South Africa between the British living in Cape Colony and the Boers, the Dutch word for farmers. The Boers had decided to create their own republic in the region of Transvaal, but tension had grown. Great Britain sent troops to the borders of Transvaal to protect British citizens. The president of the new Boer republic ordered the troops to leave within three days. When the soldiers remained, the Boer War began.

Churchill found adventure as a correspondent in South Africa.

But when it stopped so that a telegram could be sent to the commander telling him that all was well, the train was ambushed by the Boers and derailed. Facing Boer gunfire, Churchill surrendered and was taken

Nearly every country in the world has some sort of rail transportation today. If all the world's rail lines were laid end to end, they could stretch from Earth to the moon more than three times. Russia boasts the world's longest rail line. Connecting Moscow and Vladivostok, it runs about 5,600 miles (8,960 km).

to a prison camp for officers in the capital city of Pretoria. He spent his 25th birthday as a prisoner in a far-away land.

For the first three weeks of his captivity, Churchill argued with Boer officials about his release. He said he was working as a member of the press and should be freed. Boer officials countered that he gave up his rights as a member of the press when he helped some of the British evade capture.

While he continued to press for his freedom, Churchill made plans to escape. He soon found an opportunity. On December 12, when the guards' backs were turned in conversation, Churchill scaled the fence. Though he was now free, he was 300 miles (480 km) from neutral territory and on his own in a strange land. He had no map, no compass, and nothing to eat except a few chocolate bars.

Expecting to be caught, Churchill walked boldly through Pretoria. He wore a suit he purchased at the prison camp's store and a hat he stole from a minister who had also been imprisoned. Eventually Churchill stumbled upon a set of railroad tracks. He hopped aboard the first train that pulled into the station and

hid in a boxcar carrying coal sacks. Figuring officials would be searching for him on trains, he decided to jump from the car before daybreak and find a place to

Dutch farmers called Boers waited in ambush during the Boer War.

hide. Hungry, thirsty, and tired, he spent a miserably hot day hiding in a tangle of trees.

Churchill planned to ride another train through the night, but none appeared. He started walking. Quickly he realized it would take days to reach safety

A "Wanted" poster promised a reward for Winston Churchill's capture.

by foot, and he had no food. When he saw lights in the distance, he decided to try his luck and ask for help.

As he drew nearer, he realized the lights were coming from a coal mine. As luck would have it, the mine was run by two men from Scotland and two men from England. The men fed Churchill and allowed him to hide in the dark mine until the hunt for him cooled down. After several days, the men arranged transportation for Churchill.

News of Churchill's escape from the prison camp in Pretoria made headlines in Great Britain. The war had been going badly for the British, and news of his escape helped boost the country's flagging spirits. On the run, however, Churchill couldn't let anyone know his whereabouts. Because the *Morning Post* didn't hear from him, reporters throughout the British Empire began to speculate that he had been captured again or even killed. In fact, his daring escape had proved successful.

When Churchill eventually reached the safety of the British Consulate, he demanded to meet with the consul. The consul realized who his visitor was and treated him like a hero. Churchill happily accepted the offer of a hot bath, clean clothes, and a nice dinner.

News of his safe arrival quickly spread throughout the area. Churchill recalled:

Churchill spoke to an eager crowd after his escape from the Boers.

I was nearly torn to pieces by enthusiastic kindness. Whirled along on the shoulders of the crowd, I was carried to the steps of the town hall, where nothing would con-

tent them but a speech, which after a becoming reluctance I was induced to deliver.

Churchill received telegrams from around the world congratulating him on his great escape. His adventures during the war had made him an international celebrity. But he felt he could do more as an army officer. Churchill decided to rejoin the troops, and he ended up helping to free the prisoners in the Pretoria camp where he once had been held captive.

After three years of fighting, the British finally defeated the Boers. Churchill pressed the British government to show mercy to the Boers, but his commanding officers felt he had no business expressing his opinion in public. He realized that politics offered him the best way to make his opinions known, and he returned to England with new resolve.

After the war ended, several Boer generals visited England to secure aid for their devastated country. Churchill met General Louis Botha at a luncheon and told him about his capture during the war in South Africa. Botha listened quietly, then said, "Don't you recognise me? I was that man. It was I who took you prisoner." Churchill and Botha became close friends. Botha went on to become the first prime minister of the Transvaal in 1906.

5 PARLIAMENT

❧❧❧

In October 1900, Churchill tried again to gain a seat in Parliament. As before, he ran as a Conservative, following in the footsteps of his father. This time he found success. He was elected to the House of Commons, the lower house of Parliament.

Churchill had a problem, however. At the time, members of Parliament weren't paid for their service. Churchill knew he didn't have enough outside income to live comfortably. So, before he took office in February 1901, he went on a speaking tour of Great Britain and the United States. By this time he had written several books and had stories from his many adventures that he thought others would be interested in hearing.

People in Great Britain flocked to his lectures.

In 1904, Conservative member of Parliament Winston Churchill denounced his party and became a Liberal.

> *Parliament serves as the lawmaking body of Great Britain. It is made up of two houses—the lower house, called the House of Commons, and the upper house, called the House of Lords. Parliament is guided by tradition and custom as well as written law.*

Some waited in line for hours to be a part of the audience. The reaction, however, was different in the United States. Many Americans had sided with the Dutch farmers during the Boer War. Irish Americans who wanted an Ireland free of British rule didn't think kindly of Churchill either. But the experience taught him to deal with unfriendly crowds, and in the end, Churchill got what he needed. He earned around $40,000 from his lectures, enough to keep him comfortable as he began his career as an unpaid politician.

Churchill felt he had big shoes to fill. His father had served in Parliament for several years. Churchill had just published a biography of his father, and he knew his father's reputation well. Lord Randolph Churchill was remembered as a great speaker, a great politician, and a man who stuck to his beliefs, no matter the cost.

Churchill proved to be very much the same. Like his father, Churchill spoke his mind, even though his beliefs might go against his own political party. He showed this right away with his first speech in the House of Commons. Unlike other Conservatives, Churchill called for mercy for the recently conquered

Boers. On this and other issues, Churchill found himself more in agreement with the Liberals than with his own party. In time, most Conservatives had become so angry with him that they walked out

Churchill was a compelling speaker who drew large audiences.

when he rose to address the House of Commons. Churchill was upset by their display, but it didn't stop him from continuing to speak up for what he truly believed.

After four years in Parliament, Churchill clashed with his party on a trade issue and decided to switch to the Liberal Party. His timing was good. After years of being in power, the Conservatives were losing ground to the Liberals. According to the British Constitution, if the majority party loses on a major issue in the House of Commons, it must ask for a vote of confidence from the entire group. If the members of the House of Commons vote they have no confidence in the party in power, the prime minister is expected to resign. Soon after Churchill's party change, that's exactly what happened.

Sir Henry Campbell-Bannerman served in Parliament for almost 40 years. From 1905 to 1908, he served as prime minister. A member of the Liberal Party, Campbell-Bannerman advocated a policy of tolerance toward the Dutch farmers after the Boer War.

With the resignation of Conservative Prime Minister Arthur Balfour, King Edward VII asked Liberal leader Sir Henry Campbell-Bannerman to form a new government. As the new prime minister, Campbell-Bannerman chose his Cabinet. In 1905, Churchill was appointed undersecretary of state for the colonies, a high honor for one so new to Parliament. This new position wielded a great deal of power. Among his responsibilities was dealing with issues in South Africa. This meant Churchill would now be able to deal with the Boers as he liked.

In 1906, Churchill ran for reelection, this time as a Liberal. He retained his seat, and the Liberals earned a landslide majority in the House of Commons. And

Newly Liberal Churchill would often give speeches heckling his old Conservative friends in Parliament.

again Churchill was named undersecretary of state for the colonies.

In 1908, Churchill was named president of the board of trade, another Cabinet position. This new role put him in charge of much of the domestic economy. He also made changes in his personal life. In 1904, he'd met Clementine Hozier. Clementine would later remember seeing him staring at her but never approaching her to talk or dance. The two met again in 1908 and began dating. On September 12, 1908, the pair married in London's Westminster Abbey. Churchill later remarked, "I married and lived happily ever after."

Beautiful and smart, Clementine proved to be a good match for her husband. She had a lively and intelligent mind and a keen interest in politics. Together they had five children—Diana, Randolph, Sarah, Marigold, and Mary. Churchill loved his family and enjoyed spoiling his children. In 1921, Marigold unexpectedly died of a fever at the age of 3. Churchill was heartbroken, and he clung to his remaining children.

Along with spending time with his family, Churchill enjoyed eating, drinking, and playing cards. In later years, he showed a talent for painting, and many of his works of art fetched respectable prices for an amateur artist. But Churchill's first love was always politics. As a member of the House of

Clementine Hozier Churchill shared her husband's political interests.

Commons, he fought for better working conditions, regulation of the employment of children, and employment bureaus to help the unemployed find jobs. Soon he'd be fighting to maintain the security of Great Britain. ✍

6 WORLD WAR I

❦

Churchill's blood ran cold as he watched the German troops training. In 1910, he'd been named home secretary. In this role, he was in charge of the police and security. Because of his position, he was invited to Germany to observe that country's work at building up its military. What Churchill saw caused him great alarm. He observed a well-trained military and a navy that rivaled that of Great Britain. Churchill believed Germany was preparing for war, and he warned other Cabinet members of his fears.

Churchill strongly suggested that Great Britain improve its own navy to protect the country should his fears prove true. In 1911, Churchill was named first lord of the admiralty and became responsible for making specific recommendations regarding Great

Britain's navy. He quickly made his presence known, asking for faster ships, more sailors, more supplies, and better guns. He also helped create an air division within the navy. In time, this became the Royal Air Force. Churchill was among the first to see the value of airplanes as potential weapons.

On August 3, 1914, Germany declared war on France. Shortly thereafter, German troops attacked Belgium. On August 4, Great Britain declared war on Germany. World War I was under way.

Hoping to end the war quickly, Churchill developed a variety of plans. One called for the creation of an armed landship that traveled on caterpillar tracks. After convincing the prime minister of the idea's value, Churchill formed the Landships Committee of the Admiralty. From the committee's work, the world's first tank was developed.

For years, Europe had been split between two rival alliances. Germany and Austria-Hungary faced off against France, Russia, and informally, Great Britain. In June 1914, the assassination of Austria-Hungary's Archduke Franz Ferdinand provided the spark that set these rival alliances on a path toward war.

Churchill traveled to the fighting front several times, never fearing the danger of flying bullets. He never worried about public opinion either. When one plan didn't work, he'd try another despite the criticism he often heard.

One of his biggest failures came at Dardanelles, a waterway that joins

The British Mark IV tank enabled soldiers to move quickly over rugged country.

the Black Sea and the Mediterranean. Churchill believed he could send a naval task force through the Dardanelles and reach Istanbul in a day or two. He thought this move would knock Turkey out of the war and help open a seaway to Russia, one of Great Britain's allies. He was trying to find a way around the bloody stalemate of the trenches of the Western Front. The plan proved to be a dismal failure, however. Several British ships were sunk, which forced the remainder to turn back. Though the plan failed more from execution than from planning, Churchill resigned from the admiralty and decided to rejoin the army.

In November 1915, Churchill took command of an army battalion in France. His unit, the Grenadier Guards, was stationed on the front lines of battle. Life in the trenches was dangerous and miserable, but Churchill found comfort in his hobby of painting. During breaks from fighting, he painted the destruction he saw around him. He also took comfort in daily letters from home. He kept Clementine up-to-date on conditions at the front, and she shared the bigger picture, telling him what was going on in world events.

In 1916, David Lloyd George was named Great Britain's new prime minister, and Churchill returned to Parliament. He also was named to the Cabinet again, this time as minister of munitions. In this position, Churchill was charged with overseeing weapons production, delivery, and use. He spent most mornings in his London office, but in the afternoons, he usually flew to France in a private plane to meet with troops.

On April 6, 1917, the United States entered the war in support of Great Britain and the other Allies. Churchill made friends among the Americans right away by helping to equip U.S. troops. For his efforts, he became the first man from England to earn

America's Distinguished Service Medal.

American troops helped tip the scales in the Allies' favor. On November 11, 1918, World War I ended with an Allied victory. The terms of defeat were spelled out in the Treaty of Versailles, which was signed on June 28, 1919, near Paris, France. The delay between the end of the war and the signing of the treaty was caused by wrangling among the "Big Three" about what the treaty should contain.

Georges Clemenceau of France wanted Germany punished so severely it would never be able to start another war again. Germany had invaded France twice in his own lifetime, and he wanted to protect his

U.S. troops marched through London on their way to join the Allies.

country against German aggression.

U.S. President Woodrow Wilson also wished to see Germany punished, but he hoped a way could be found to heal the wounds the war had caused in Europe.

The last of the Big Three, David Lloyd George of Great Britain wanted to see Germany punished as well, but his primary fear was the spread of communism outside of Russia. The British prime minister feared Germany might turn to communism if its government signed a treaty its citizens felt was too harsh. He was also very aware that bringing Germany back into the European economy was an important step in postwar economic recovery. However, he realized that his political career would quickly come to an end if he appeared too lenient with the Germans.

Like his prime minister, Churchill feared the spread of communism. He also held true to his conviction that defeated nations should be treated with compassion. He suggested that Great Britain send several ships loaded with food to Germany to help ease the suffering there. Churchill recalled:

My own mood was divided between anxiety for the future and desire to help the fallen foe. The conversation ran on the great qualities of the German people, on the tremendous fight they had made against three-quarters of the world, on the impossibility of rebuilding Europe except with their aid. At that time we thought they were actually starving. … I suggested that we should immediately, pending further news, rush a dozen great ships crammed with provisions into Hamburg.

The Hall of Mirrors was crowded with spectators watching the signing of the Treaty of Versailles.

Though the prime minister may have agreed with Churchill's feelings about leniency, he knew British citizens, angry about the war, would never stand for it.

In the end, the Treaty of Versailles forced Germany to admit it was entirely responsible for the start of World War I. As such, it was held responsible for paying for the damages. The amount of reparations Germany was expected to pay wasn't spelled out in the treaty. When the Allies eventually came up with

France held German prisoners behind barbed wire until the end of the war.

a figure, it amounted to about $33 billion, a figure that not only financially crippled Germany but also proved impossible to pay.

The treaty also limited the German army to 100,000 men and forbade the formation of an air force and the possession of tanks. Germany's naval capabilities were held to six battleships and no submarines. In addition, Germany was stripped of more than 13 percent of its territory, although most of the land Germany lost was inhabited by non-Germans. Portions were given to France, Belgium, Denmark, Poland, and Czechoslovakia.

Germans found the Treaty of Versailles harsh and humiliating, but the Allies felt they had made a fair agreement. The Allies planned to invade Germany if the Germans failed to sign the treaty.

Those involved in designing the treaty hoped it would end any chance of another world war. However, the treaty didn't secure peace in Europe. It left Germany embarrassed and financially unstable, which only led to more problems.

With the war ended, many in Great Britain wanted to disarm. Churchill, however, warned against it. Unlike many others, he didn't believe that World War I would be the last war Great Britain would fight. He asked that the country's weapons be stored. In time, his forward thinking would prove vital to his country's survival. ❧

Chapter 7 WARNINGS OF A SECOND WAR

ༀ

Just six years after the end of World War I, Churchill began warning Parliament about Germany again. He believed that German nationalists were determined to overturn the Treaty of Versailles and bring Germany to a position of dominance in Europe. He said:

> The enormous contingents of German youth growing to military manhood year by year are inspired by the fiercest sentiments and the soul of Germany smoulders with dreams of a war of liberation or revenge.

Churchill found his warnings ignored. The British were still weary from World War I, and they didn't see the danger posed by what they viewed as a suffering, humiliated Germany.

After the end of World War I, Churchill held several important government positions, including serving as chancellor of the exchequer. In this role, he had reached the same position within the government that his father had held in the 1880s, and in fact, he was sworn in wearing his father's old robes.

In 1924, Churchill again joined the Conservative Party, but with the fall of the Conservative government in 1929, he lost his Cabinet position. For the next decade, he would remain a member of Parliament, though largely ignored and frustrated. He found some comfort by spending his free time lecturing and writing.

In 1931, during a lecture tour of the United States, Churchill went to visit a friend in New York. Forgetting that Americans drive on the right side of the road, unlike the British who drive on the left, Churchill walked into traffic and was struck by a taxi. Again, Churchill survived, lending support to his long-standing belief that he had a higher purpose he had yet to discover and for which he had again been spared.

After being hospitalized, Churchill spent a few days in the Bahamas to finish recovering before completing his lecture tour. When he came back to Great Britain, he started working on a book about his ancestor the first Duke of Marlborough. The duke

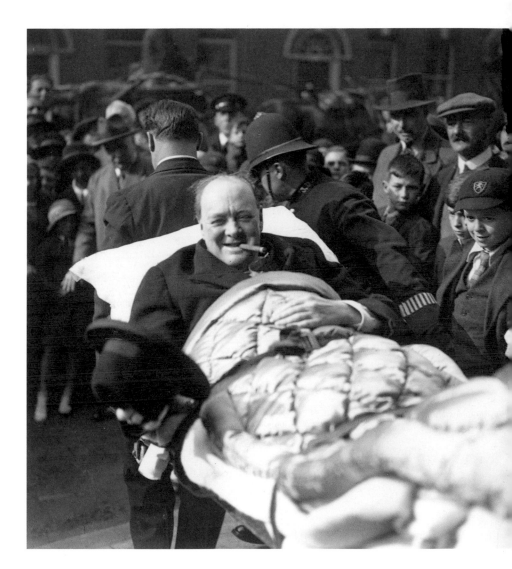

was known as a great general and diplomat. In 1705, the English government built him Blenheim Palace, where Churchill had lived as a boy, in recognition of the duke's service to his country.

After recovering from his accident, Churchill left the hospital to a crowd of onlookers.

With plenty of time on his hands, Churchill

traveled extensively to research the biography. Among the places he went was Munich, Germany. He was able to learn more about the duke, but he also started hearing disturbing rumblings about a man named Adolf Hitler and the Nazi party. Churchill tried to learn all he could, and he shared his findings with others in Parliament. Still, few listened to him, even after Hitler came to power in 1933.

One person who did listen and appreciated his efforts was a man named Sir Henry Strakosch, a gold mining executive. Strakosch provided Churchill with information on German economic and military rearmament, as well as Hitler's increasingly public hatred and persecution of Jews. Strakosch hoped other British citizens would also begin listening to Churchill. For Churchill's efforts, Strakosch rewarded him by helping him with his debts.

Churchill was right to be concerned about Adolf Hitler, especially concerning his treatment of the Jews. Around 6 million Jews would be killed by Hitler and the Nazis in the concentration camps of World War II.

In 1922, Churchill had purchased a beautiful estate in Kent called Chartwell. His family had moved many times over the past decade, and he was delighted to be able to give them a permanent home. After a world economic depression hit in 1929, he was finding it difficult to keep up with the

expense of running the estate. He had decided to sell Chartwell until Strakosch stepped forward in 1938 with financial assistance.

Churchill's estate, Chartwell, was the first permanent home his family had known.

Churchill kept pressure on the House of Commons to listen to him, but the majority in Parliament wanted peace at nearly any price. On March 7, 1936, against the terms of the Treaty of Versailles, Hitler ordered

Despite his hectic schedule, Churchill found time for his children Randolph and Diana.

the German army to march into the Rhineland, a strip of land separating Germany from France. No one stopped him. Two years later, on March 12, 1938, German troops overtook Austria without a shot being fired.

Next, Hitler set his sights on Czechoslovakia. On September 15, 1938, Prime Minister Neville Chamberlain traveled to Germany for the first of a series of meetings with Hitler. During the course of the meetings, the German dictator assured Chamberlain that he only wanted the Sudetenland, a part of Czechoslovakia mainly populated by Germans. By appeasing Hitler's wish and granting him Sudetenland, Chamberlain believed the German dictator would be satisfied. Chamberlain returned to Great Britain confident he had secured peace for Europe. Churchill was among the few who knew better. Of Chamberlain's deal with Hitler, he said:

> *We have sustained a great defeat without a war, the consequences of which will travel far with us. And do not suppose that this is the end. This is only the beginning of the reckoning.*

Time proved Churchill right. In March 1939, all of Czechoslovakia fell to Germany. At the end of the month, Great Britain and France offered a warning to Hitler. They'd come to Poland's aid if Germany dared attack it. After securing a nonaggression agreement with Russia in August, Germany pounced on Poland in September. True to their words, Great Britain and France declared war on Germany. World War II had begun. ✍

8 WARTIME PRIME MINISTER

Chapter

❦

By 1940, the Liberal majority in the House of Commons had fallen from 200 to 80, and Neville Chamberlain resigned as prime minister. On May 10, Churchill took his place. At age 65, he was in the right position, place, and time to do what he had always believed he was meant to do.

On May 13, he addressed the House of Commons in a famous speech that gave the worried nation courage. He offered his "blood, toil, tears, and sweat," and called for "victory at all costs." He showed his fellow citizens he had confidence and hope, and it rubbed off on them, too.

But the Germans had been moving quickly. On the same day Churchill took over as prime minister, Germany attacked the Netherlands, Luxembourg,

Prime Minister Winston Churchill stood on a tank to receive his army's salute during an inspection of the Eastern Command Armored Division in 1942.

Benito Mussolini
ruled Italy for more
than 20 years, most of
that time as a dicta-
tor. He originated a
form of government
called fascism, which
is marked by total gov-
ernment control of all
areas of human affairs.
Mussolini sought to
make Italy a major
world power and to cre-
ate an Italian colonial
empire. Instead, he led
his nation to defeat in
World War II and was
killed by his own citi-
zens before the end of
the war.

and Belgium. Hitler had also added a new ally—Benito Mussolini, the leader of Italy.

As French and British forces marched to challenge the Germans in Belgium, they found themselves encircled in a German trap. Their only options were to surrender or to retreat to the sea. They chose the latter and raced to the French port of Dunkirk on the English Channel.

From May 26 until June 4, the Allies mounted a massive evacuation. More than 800 sea-going vessels of various kinds—from warships to private yachts—sailed between the coasts of France and Great Britain in the rescue effort. Two hundred twenty-six British boats were sunk under heavy fire, but more than 338,000 soldiers—the majority of the British army—were evacuated. However, all their tanks and equipment had to be left behind. Churchill's foresight after World War I saved the day. Despite the loss of weapons and other equipment, Great Britain still had all the weapons Churchill made sure were saved after the war. The equipment may

Hundreds of thousands of Allied troops were evacuated from the French port of Dunkirk.

have been outdated, but it was needed after such a huge loss at Dunkirk.

On June 5, Hitler launched an offensive against France, ultimately forcing its surrender. Hitler expected the British to seek peace rather than fight alone, but he was wrong. Churchill was determined to battle Hitler and hoped the United States would come to his aid.

Even before the fall of France, Churchill knew help was needed to defeat Hitler and the Nazis. On May 18, he'd sent a message to President Franklin Roosevelt with the hope the United States would help. He told Roosevelt:

> *I do not need to tell you about the gravity of what has happened. We are determined to persevere to the very end, whatever the result of the great battle raging in France may be. We must expect in any case to be attacked here ... before very long, and we hope to give a good account of ourselves. But if American assistance is to play any part it must be available soon.*

Roosevelt responded that he had to respect the wishes of Congress and the American public to remain neutral.

With Great Britain refusing to surrender, Hitler made plans to cross the English Channel and invade the island empire. First, however, he knew he had to establish air superiority. That meant defeating the Royal Air Force, known as the RAF.

In July 1940, the Battle of Britain began. It marked the first full-scale air battle in the history of warfare. While the German air force, the Luftwaffe, boasted more planes than the RAF, the British had the advantage of fighting at home. If a German pilot survived after being shot down over Great Britain, he usually became a prisoner, but if a British pilot survived being shot down, he lived to fly for England another day. The British also produced the best fighter plane of its time, the Spitfire. British pilots shot down nearly twice as many planes as the

Spitfires flew in formation as part of Allied operations in North Africa.

Germans did.

Despite the RAF's dominance in the air, the Luftwaffe continued to inflict pain on the British people. Hoping to pound the British into surrendering, the Germans bombed London and other cities nearly every night during the fall and winter of 1940–1941. Churchill often visited neighborhoods ravaged by the blasts. In one instance, more than 1,000 people crowded around him and cheered in support of him despite the fact many had lost their homes. Churchill wept openly in admiration of their spirit.

When air bombing failed to bring Great Britain to its knees, Hitler scrapped plans for Operation Sea Lion—an invasion of the island via the English Channel. Churchill knew the men of the RAF had saved Great Britain. "Never in the field of human conflict was so much owed by so many to so few," Churchill said in praise of the RAF in the House of Commons.

Great Britain also was looking at a mounting debt owed to American factories. Despite its talk of neutrality, the United States sold vital supplies to Great Britain but not to Germany. When Great Britain found itself facing a shortage of cash to pay for much-needed goods, the U.S. Congress passed the Lend-Lease Act in March 1941. This program allowed Allies to purchase American goods without

Churchill (left) was met with a cheering crowd as he toured a bomb-damaged area of Manchester.

a timetable for payment.

Still, Churchill persisted in asking for more help. After months of exchanging letters and phone calls, Churchill and President Roosevelt finally met face to face on August 9, 1941, in Placentia Bay, off the coast of Newfoundland. A lasting friendship developed, but Roosevelt still avoided any promise of using U.S. troops to fight the war.

Everything changed, however, on December 7, 1941. The Japanese, one of the Axis powers fighting

Churchill, Roosevelt, and Stalin (seated left to right) met to discuss the end of the war.

From February 4 to 11, 1945, World War II's "Big Three" Allied leaders met in Yalta, a resort along the Black Sea, to discuss the terms they'd find acceptable at the conclusion of the war. Churchill

wanted a free, democratic Europe. Stalin wanted to protect his borders so that he wouldn't face attack again. Roosevelt wanted to finish the war with Japan and was willing to compromise with Stalin to secure peace.

With the largest army in Europe, Stalin was able to get his way at Yalta. Roosevelt and Churchill agreed that all Soviet prisoners of war who left the country on their own be returned to the Soviet Union. They also agreed to allow Soviet troops to remain in Poland until order was restored and free elections could be arranged. While Roosevelt and Churchill remained true to their words, Stalin didn't. Soviet troops remained in Poland, as well as eastern Germany and other countries.

With Winston Churchill and the Soviet Union's Joseph Stalin, U.S. President Franklin Delano Roosevelt was the third member of World War II's "Big Three." Roosevelt served the United States as president for more than 12 years. He led the United States through two monumental events—the Great Depression and World War II. Though some disagreed with the large role he gave the federal government, his programs and policies marked him as a friend and protector of the "common man."

9 AFTER THE WAR

❧❧❧

In 1945, just weeks before the end of the war, Great Britain held its general election. Churchill was stunned when he lost reelection as prime minister on July 26, even though he had been instrumental in leading the Allies to victory. But Great Britain saw Churchill and his Cabinet as a wartime government, and people now wanted a peacetime prime minister. But Churchill maintained his seat in Parliament, and he kept his hurt feelings from the public.

As a member of the House of Commons, Churchill again shared words of warning. He saw a new threat on the horizon—the communists in the Soviet Union. Despite working with Stalin as an ally during the war, Churchill knew he couldn't trust the Soviet leader. He worried that while the world decided what to do with

Longtime British Prime Minister Winston Churchill posed for a formal portrait in 1956.

President Franklin Delano Roosevelt died on April 12, 1945, before the end of World War II. Vice President Harry Truman became president and made the decision to drop atomic bombs on the Japanese cities of Hiroshima and Nagasaki. Together, these bombings killed as many as 140,000 people. Thousands more died of radiation sickness. The bombings prompted Japan's surrender, and on September 2, 1945, World War II officially ended.

the defeated Germany, the Soviet Union would begin grabbing up land in Europe. While many thought his fears were unfounded, Churchill continued to issue warnings—just as he had before and after Hitler came to power.

Though many disagreed with Churchill, he was still highly respected. He received many honorary degrees from colleges and universities around the world and continued to be much in demand as a speaker. When he traveled to Westminster College in Fulton, Missouri, on March 5, 1946, he gave what proved to be one his most famous speeches—the "Iron Curtain" speech. In it, he talked about the danger the Soviet Union posed to freedom and world peace. He said:

From Stettin in the Baltic to Trieste in the Adriatic an iron curtain has descended across the continent. Behind that line lie all the capitals of the ancient states of Central and Eastern Europe. The Communist parties, which were very small in all these Eastern States of Europe, have been raised to pre-eminence and power far beyond

their numbers and are seeking everywhere to obtain totalitarian control. Police government is prevailing in nearly every case, and so far, except in Czechoslovakia, there is no true democracy.

Churchill spoke to the Congress of Europe about a closer relationship among the countries of Europe.

But Churchill would again find his warning unheeded. A war-weary world didn't want to fight another enemy. The Cold War developed between the Soviet Union and the Western nations. Though it didn't involve actual fighting, it did involve mistrust and fear between communist and noncommunist nations. It seemed that at any moment another world war could break out. And war now seemed more dangerous than ever. The United States had dropped two atomic bombs on Japan to bring World War II to a close. From those moments on, nuclear war became a threat the people of the world lived with every day.

Churchill made sure the world would never forget the lessons of the last war by writing a six-volume history of World War II. Freed from his duties as prime minister, he also worked on his home. He enlarged Chartwell to include a dairy and a stable for racehorses, one of his passions. He also built and stocked fishponds on his property and found time to indulge in his hobby of painting. But he found nothing as satisfying as being a politician.

In 1951, British voters returned the Conservatives to power, and in October, the 76-year-old Churchill took on the title of prime minister for a second time. Though he tackled issues ranging from helping the country's continued recovery from World War II to securing peace for the future, his second term didn't prove as remarkable as the first.

Perhaps his most remarkable year, on a personal

level, was 1953. Though he'd turned down the offer several years before, in 1953, Churchill accepted knighthood. He was awarded the Order of the Garter,

Throughout his life, Churchill enjoyed painting and sold many of his works.

the oldest and highest order of knighthood in Great Britain. As he knelt before her, Queen Elizabeth II dubbed him Sir Winston Churchill.

That same year, he also earned the highest possible recognition for his work as a writer. A best-selling author with several exhaustive studies of history and people to his credit, Churchill was awarded the Nobel Prize in literature. Because he was attending an international conference with the Americans and French, Churchill was unable to accept his prize in person. Instead his wife, Clementine, read the speech he had prepared. In a show of unusual humility, Churchill wrote that he hoped he was worthy to be included among the many talented writers who had won the award in the past. He wrote:

> *I am proud but also, I must admit, awe-struck at your decision to include me. I do hope you are right. I feel we are both running a considerable risk and that I do not deserve it. But I shall have no misgivings if you have none.*

On March 5, 1953, Joseph Stalin died. Two months later, Churchill gave a speech demanding the end of the Cold War. Again, his message was largely ignored. Though some may have agreed with him, the Cold War would continue for decades to come.

As Churchill grew older, his health began to fail.

In the summer of 1949, he had suffered a mild stroke. The event left no visible effects and happened while Churchill was on vacation. The public didn't even hear about the episode.

Churchill and his wife, Clementine, attended many events in his honor.

> *Most strokes are caused by blood clots that prevent the flow of blood to victims' brains. Since blood carries oxygen and important nutrients, disruption of blood flow to a person's brain can cause permanent damage or even death.*

He wasn't as fortunate the second time. In June 1953, a more serious stroke partially paralyzed him and took away his ability to speak. Ever the fighter, Churchill worked hard to learn to walk and talk again. In time, he succeeded, but the path to recovery was paved with great frustration. "I was always rather weepy, but now I have turned into a real cry-baby," he said. "Is there nothing to be done about it?"

By September, Churchill recovered enough to allow himself to be seen in public again, but his health continued to deteriorate. He was only able to work a few hours a day, and his mind wasn't always clear. Some members of his Cabinet suggested he resign. On April 5, 1955, he followed their advice. He retired as prime minister, though he continued to hold a seat in Parliament. While he continued to speak outside the House of Commons, inside he held his tongue. He listened from the seat of honor—a corner seat on the center aisle set aside for prominent rebels.

Churchill was reelected to Parliament in 1955 and 1959, but poor health continued to plague him, and he retired from the House of Commons in 1964. More strokes were on the horizon. The final one came in January 1965. Churchill had once quipped,

"I am ready to meet my Maker. Whether my Maker is prepared for the great ordeal of meeting me is another matter." On January 24, 1965, the 70th anniversary of

Winston Churchill welcomed Queen Elizabeth II to his retirement dinner.

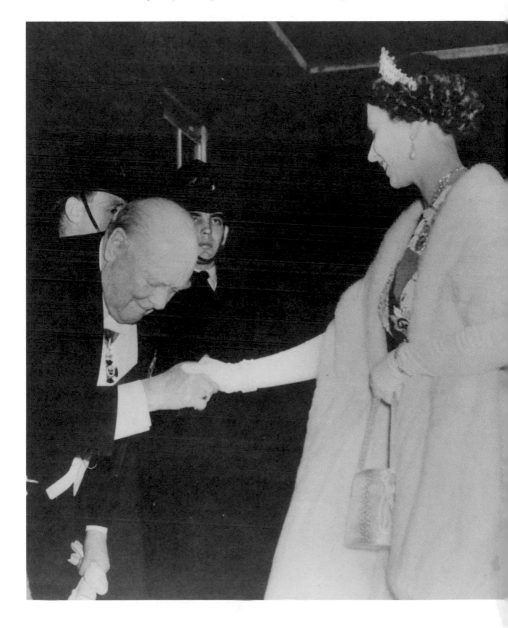

Winston Churchill's funeral procession traveled through the streets of London.

the death of his father, 90-year-old Winston Churchill died. All Great Britain mourned.

After word of Churchill's death reached her, Queen Elizabeth II sent a message to his widow, Clementine. She wrote:

The whole world is the poorer by the loss of his many-sided genius, while the survival of this country and the sister nations of the Commonwealth, in the face of the greatest danger that has ever threatened them, will be a perpetual memorial to his leadership, his vision, and his indomitable courage.

Elizabeth II became queen in 1952 after the death of her father, King George VI. Still reigning today, Queen Elizabeth II has four children, including Prince Charles, the heir to the throne.

At his own insistence, Churchill was buried alongside his parents in a village cemetery near the palace where he had lived as a boy.

Winston Churchill is remembered as a visionary and a fearless wartime leader. He knew the dangers a devastated Germany and a leader like Hitler posed to the world. Churchill possessed the courage to continually warn others, even when they didn't want to listen. And when his warnings proved true, he led his country against Hitler's tyranny, even when Great Britain was forced to fight alone.

CHURCHILL'S LIFE

1874

Born November 30
in his grandfather's
palace in Blenheim,
England

1896

Serves as a
lieutenant
in the 4th
Hussars in
India

1898

In September,
takes part
in the Battle
of Omdurman
in Sudan

1885

1876

Alexander Graham
Bell uses the first
telephone to speak
to his assistant,
Thomas Watson

1896

The Olympic Games are held
for the first time in recent
history in Athens, Greece

WORLD EVENTS

1900

Elected to
Parliament as a
Conservative

1899

Captured during
the Boer War in
South Africa but
later escapes

1901

Embarks on
lecture tour of
Great Britain
and the United
States before
taking a seat
in the House
of Commons

1903

Brothers Orville
and Wilbur Wright
successfully fly a
powered airplane

1901

First exhibition
of Pablo Picasso
opens

1900

First rigid
dirigible is built
by Ferdinand
von Zeppelin

CHURCHILL'S LIFE

1906
Reelected to Parliament as a Liberal

1908
Becomes president of the board of trade; marries Clementine Hozier

1911
Becomes first lord of the admiralty

1910

1909
The National Association for the Advancement of Colored People (NAACP) is founded

1914
Archduke Franz Ferdinand is assassinated, launching World War I (1914–1918)

WORLD EVENTS

1924

Rejoins
Conservative
Party; appointed
chancellor of
the exchequer

1929

Loses Cabinet
position and
spends next
decade largely
removed from
politics

1940

Becomes prime
minister on
May 10

1926

Claude Monet
and Mary Cassat,
well-known
impressionist
painters, die

1939

German troops invade Poland;
Britain and France declare war
on Germany; World War II
(1939–1945) begins

CHURCHILL'S LIFE

1945

Meets with Allied leaders in Yalta to decide terms for ending World War II

1951

Becomes prime minister for second time

1953

Wins the Nobel Prize in Literature; accepts knighthood from Queen Elizabeth II; suffers a stroke that forces him to learn to walk and talk again

1950

1949

Birth of the People's Republic of China

1951

Libya gains its independence with help from the United Nations

1953

The first Europeans climb Mount Everest

WORLD EVENTS

1955

Resigns as prime
minister April 5
but remains in
Parliament

1964

Retires from
Parliament

1965

Dies January 24

1960

1959

Fidel Castro
becomes leader
of Cuba

1963

Kenya becomes an
independent republic
with Jomo Kenyatta
as its first president

DATE OF BIRTH: November 30, 1874

BIRTHPLACE: Blenheim, England

FATHER: Lord Randolph Churchill
(1849–1895)

MOTHER: Jennie Jerome Churchill
(1854–1921)

EDUCATION: Graduated from the
Royal Military College
at Sandhurst

SPOUSE: Clementine Hozier
Churchill (1885–1977)

DATE OF MARRIAGE: September 12, 1908

CHILDREN: Diana (1909–1963)
Randolph (1911–1968)
Sarah (1914–1982)
Marigold (1918–1921)
Mary (1922–)

DATE OF DEATH: January 24, 1965

PLACE OF BURIAL: St. Martin's Churchyard,
Oxfordshire, England

FURTHER READING

Adams, Simon. *Winston Churchill*. Austin: Raintree Steck-Vaughn Publishers, 2003.

Binns, Tristan Boyer. *Winston Churchill: Soldier and Politician*. New York: Franklin Watts, 2004.

Gavin, Philip. *World War II in Europe*. San Diego: Lucent Books, 2004.

Hynson, Colin. *World War II: A Primary Source History*. Milwaukee: Gareth Stevens, 2005.

MacDonald, Fiona. *Winston Churchill*. Milwaukee: World Almanac Library, 2003.

LOOK FOR MORE SIGNATURE LIVES BOOKS ABOUT THIS ERA:

Benazir Bhutto: *Pakistani Prime Minister and Activist*
ISBN 0-7565-1578-5

Fidel Castro: *Leader of Communist Cuba*
ISBN 0-7565-1580-7

Jane Goodall: *Legendary Primatologist*
ISBN 0-7565-1590-4

Adolf Hitler: *Dictator of Nazi Germany*
ISBN 0-7565-1589-0

Eva Perón: *First Lady of Argentina*
ISBN 0-7565-1585-8

Queen Noor: *American-born Queen of Jordan*
ISBN 0-7565-1595-5

Joseph Stalin: *Dictator of the Soviet Union*
ISBN 0-7565-1597-1

On the Web

For more information on *Winston Churchill*, use FactHound.

1. Go to *www.facthound.com*
2. Type in a search word related to this book or this book ID: 0756515823
3. Click on the *Fetch It* button.

FactHound will fetch the best Web sites for you.

Historic Site

Winston Churchill Memorial and Library
501 Westminster Ave.
Fulton, MO 65251
573/592-5234
Museum and library dedicated to the memory of Winston Churchill

flogging
a beating with a whip or a stick

fortification
the act of strengthening a place against attack

governess
a woman who cares for and supervises a child,
especially in a private household

graft
a medical procedure in which skin is taken from
one place to heal an injury on another

infantry
soldiers who fight on foot

Parliament
the part of the British government that
makes laws

pensions
regular payments to retired people

polo
a game played on horseback by two teams of four
players; the players try to hit a small ball using
long, wooden mallets

reparations
payment made by a defeated nation to a victorious
nation for wartime damages or expenses

shilling
a British coin under the old monetary system

totalitarian
complete control by the government

vindicate
to free from blame

Source Notes

Chapter 1

Page 9, line 5: Christian Graf von Krockow. *Churchill: Man of the Century*. London: London House, 2000, p. 123.

Page 10, line 13: Ibid., p 122.

Page 10, sidebar: Winston Churchill Quotes. 21 Nov. 2005. http://www. brainyquote.com/quotes/ authors/w/winston_churchill.html

Chapter 2

Page 15, line 6: John B. Severance. *Winston Churchill: Soldier, Statesman, Artist*. New York: Clarion Books, 1996, p. 14.

Page 15, line 22: Winston Churchill. *My Early Life*. New York: Simon & Schuster, 1996, p. 3.

Page 18, line 9: *Churchill: Man of the Century*, p. 16.

Page 18, line 25: *Winston Churchill: Soldier, Statesman, Artist*, p. 15.

Chapter 3

Page 26, line 28: *My Early Life*, p. 62.

Page 27, line 9: Ibid.

Page 29, line 5: Ibid., p. 72.

Chapter 4

Page 35, line 16: *Churchill: Man of the Century*, p. 23.

Page 37, line 15: *My Early Life*, pp. 197–198.

Page 44, line 1: Ibid., p. 297.

Page 45, sidebar: Ibid., p. 253.

Chapter 5

Page 52, line 12: J.E. Driemen. *An Unbreakable Spirit: Winston Churchill*. Minneapolis: Dillon Press, Inc., 1990, p. 56.

Chapter 6

Page 61: *Churchill: Man of the Century*, pp. 62–63.

Chapter 7

Page 65, line 6: John Lukacs. *Churchill: Visionary, Statesman, Historian*. New Haven, Conn.: Yale University Press, 2002, p. 5.

Page 71, line 14: Joshua Rubenstein. *Adolf Hitler*. New York: Franklin Watts, 1982, p. 71.

Chapter 8

Page 73, lines 9–10: *Churchill: Man of the Century*, p. 123.

Page 76, line 9: Ibid., p. 130.

Page 78, line 17: Ibid., p. 140.

Page 80, line 28: Leonard Wibberley. *The Life of Winston Churchill*. New York: Farrar, Straus and Cudahy, Inc., 1956, p. 189.

Chapter 9

Page 86, line 22: Ibid., p. 204.

Page 90, line 15: Winston Churchill. "Nobel Prize Acceptance Speech." 10 Nov. 2005. http://nobelprize.org/literature/laureates/1953/churchill-speech.html

Page 93, line 1: *Churchill: Man of the Century*, p. 203.

Page 92, line 27: *Winston Churchill: Soldier, Statesman, Artist*, p. 131.

Page 95, line 1: *New York Times*. 10 Nov. 2005. http://www.nytimes.com/learning/general/onthisday/bday/1130.html

Select Bibliography

BBC History. 10 Nov. 2005. http://www.bbc.co.uk/history/historic_figures/churchill_winston.shtml

The Churchill Centre. 10 Nov. 2005. http://www.winstonchurchill.org/i4a/pages/index.cfm?pageid=1

Churchill, Winston. *My Early Life.* New York: Simon & Schuster, 1996.

Driemen, J.E. *An Unbreakable Spirit: Winston Churchill.* Minneapolis: Dillon Press, Inc., 1990.

Library of Congress. 10 Nov. 2005. http://www.loc.gov/exhibits/churchill

Lukacs, John. *Churchill: Visionary, Statesman, Historian.* New Haven, Conn.: Yale University Press, 2002.

Nobelprize.org. 10 Nov. 2005. http://nobelprize.org/literature/laureates/1953/churchill-bio.html

Severance, John B. *Winston Churchill: Soldier, Statesman, Artist.* New York: Clarion Books, 1996.

Time Magazine Online. 10 Nov. 2005. http://www.time.com/time/time100/leaders/profile/churchill.html

Toland, John. *Adolf Hitler, Volume II.* Garden City, New York: Doubleday & Company, Inc., 1976.

von Krockow, Christian Graf. *Churchill: Man of the Century.* London: London House, 2000.

Wibberley, Leonard. *The Life of Winston Churchill.* New York: Farrar, Straus and Cudahy, Inc., 1956.

Brenda Haugen started in the newspaper business and had a career as an award-winning journalist before finding her niche as an author. Since then, she has written and edited many books, most of them for children. A graduate of the University of North Dakota in Grand Forks, Brenda lives in North Dakota with her family.

Image Credits

Bettmann/Corbis, cover (top), 4–5, 39, 70; Carl Mydans/Time Life Pictures/Getty Images Inc., cover (bottom), 2, 84; AFP/Getty Images, 8, 99 (top right); Reg Speller/Getty Images, 11; Hulton Archive/Getty Images, 12, 14, 15, 20, 22, 25, 28, 36, 42, 44, 54, 57, 64, 75, 96 (top right); General Photographic Agency/Getty Images, 17; Michael Freeman/Corbis, 19, 96 (top left); Library of Congress, 27, 53, 77, 93, 96 (bottom left), 98 (top right), 99 (bottom right), 101 (top left and bottom, all); Corbis, 30, 97 (top); Time Life Pictures/Pictures Inc./Getty Images, 33; Van Hoepen/ Hulton Archive/Getty Images, 41; Ernest H. Mills/Getty Images, 46, 98 (top left); Central Press/Getty Images, 49, 89; Mary Evans Picture Library, 51; DVIC/NARA, 59, 61, 62, 82, 100 (top); Chris Ware/Keystone/Getty Images, 67; Time Life Pictures/Getty Images, 69, 99 (top left); Fox Photos/Hulton Archive/Getty Images, 72, 94, 101 (top right); Keystone/Getty Images, 79; Kurt Hutton/Picture Post/Getty Images, 87; Central Press/Hulton Archive/ Getty Images, 91; Compass Point Books, 96 (bottom right); NASA, 97 (bottom); Underwood & Underwood/DVIC/NARA, 98 (bottom); Corel, 99 (bottom left), 100 (bottom right); Brand X Pictures, 100 (bottom left).